SUNSET - A COLLECTION OF POEMS

APOORV SAXENA

ISBN 979-888629300-5

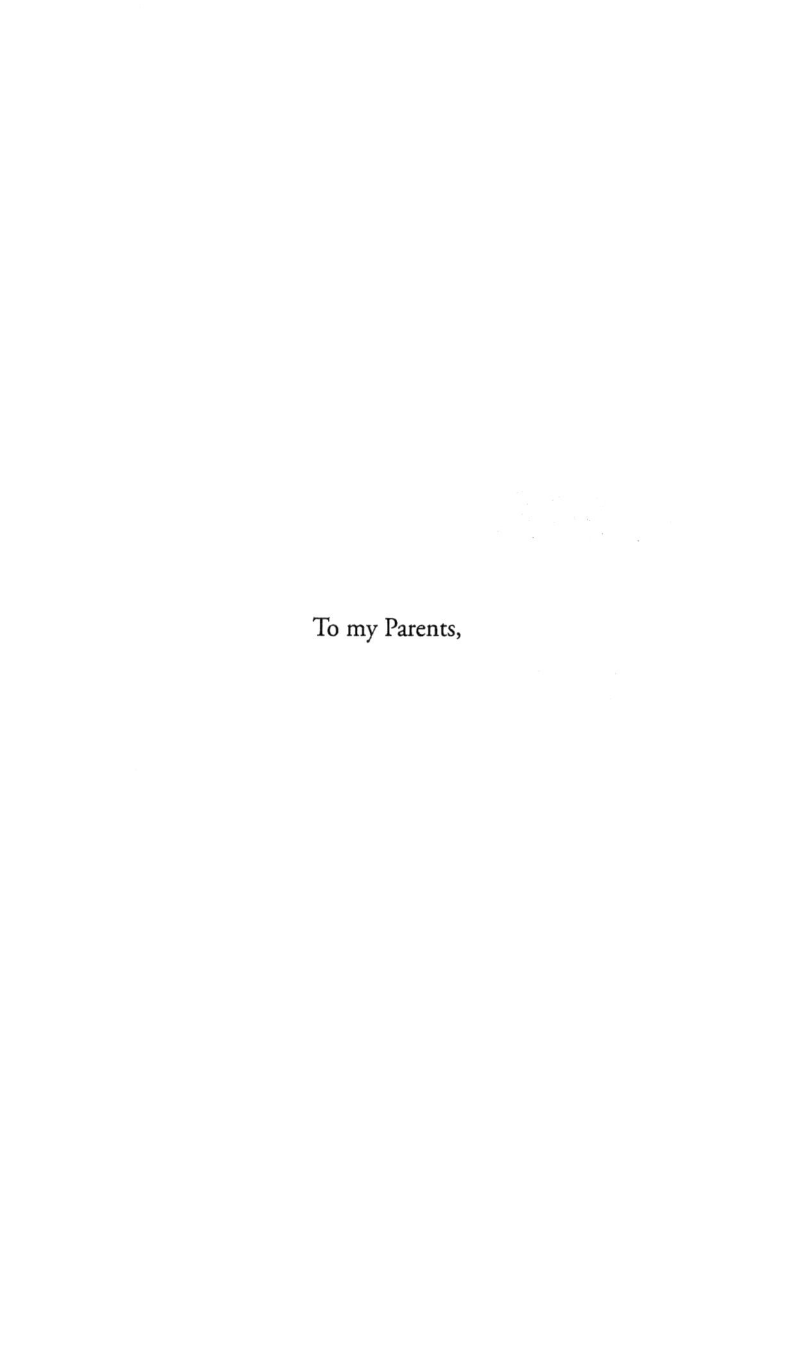

To my Parents,

Contents

Preface ix
1. Chapter 1 1
2. Chapter 2 2
3. Chapter 3 3
4. Chapter 4 4
5. Chapter 5 5
6. Chapter 6 6
7. Chapter 7 7
8. Chapter 8 8
9. Chapter 9 9
10. Chapter 10 10
11. Chapter 11 11
12. Chapter 12 12
13. Chapter 13 13
14. Chapter 14 14
15. Chapter 15 15
16. Chapter 16 16
17. Chapter 17 17
18. Chapter 18 18
19. Chapter 19 19
20. Chapter 20 20
21. Chapter 21 21
22. Chapter 22 22
23. Chapter 23 23

Contents

24. Chapter 24 24
25. Chapter 25 25
26. Chapter 26 26
27. Chapter 27 27
28. Chapter 28 28
29. Chapter 29 29
30. Chapter 30 30
31. Chapter 31 31
32. Chapter 32 32
33. Chapter 33 33
34. Chapter 34 34
35. Chapter 35 35
36. Chapter 36 36
37. Chapter 37 37
38. Chapter 38 38
39. Chapter 39 39
40. Chapter 40 40
41. Chapter 41 41
42. Chapter 42 42
43. Chapter 43 43
44. Chapter 44 44
45. Chapter 45 45
46. Chapter 46 46
47. Chapter 47 47

Contents

48. Chapter 48 48
49. Chapter 49 49
50. Chapter 50 50
51. Chapter 51 51
52. Chapter 52 52
53. Chapter 53 53

Preface

I have found poetry the best way to express myself; whenever I feel overwhelmed or underwhelmed, I reside to poetry. It has provided me with strength and has helped me to express myself from the most trying time to the most undemanding ones.

Chapter1

Every day looks monotonous same as it was yesterday
But these monotonous routines are blessings
Things shift slowly like a river cuts mountains
Despite all the storms, things grow again
Some Incidents comes in a wave one after another
Some are good, and some are bad, some are silent some are not
Let's enjoy the beauty of whatever comes in our way
Do whatever is there to happen, not disheartened by things to come.

Chapter2

Amid your lowest days
In times when you expect a lot from others
In times when you feel down, doubtful, apologetic
In those times, hold on to yourself
In those times, remember your grin
In those times, remember nothing is constant, and this is also not constant
From time to time, just fall for your soul sometimes
In times do remember how many people stand with you and count yourself to
It's all struggle, frustration and everything Imperfect, making it Worthwhile.

Chapter3

Sometimes coming out of pain, Looks like pain itself,
Sometimes it's not your choice but necessary to leave things behind,
In those times, remember, "This shall too pass."
In those times, don't let your sleep & peace be a stranger
Let the new you replace the old
These new which enshrined all the learning from the old
A place where you belongs to yourself
A place where you can't relate to the old.

Chapter4

It's hard to accept something a lot of times
At 3:00 AM in the morning, thinking it was yours
the next second you realize it was all for nothing
It's hard to accept how it could end this way
you wanted it to happen
You gave all you have
what you got is a memory
it's hard to accept it, but what if you don't take it
Time is passing by, and it would be harder later
The sun is out.

Chapter5

Tides are changing; you can not stop them
There might be something better on the other side
They will take old things from the shore and bring the new stuff back
Then it will wait and repeat itself over and over
Whatever happened in the past tides does not matter now
The change with tides won't matter after some time
Trying to change it and looking back won't make a grain of difference to them
So why do we look back all the time? Does it change anything?
The tide has come and gone
waiting for the next day now, to start all over again.

Chapter6

We have three life's all in one soul and one body that co-exists
Whether it's private, public or personal, it should live and be loved by us
Let these three different lives not fight with each other
Being in conflict with these lives just bring suffering all along
Those lives not compatible with each other living along
Trying to find the harmony in between reflects the common dream it has
Being in peace with each other in their natural state
when they die, they all die together still they fight like there are hundred lives to live

Chapter7

Hope you can hear yourself without saying anything
Not failing to listen to yourself when it's needed
Not waking up and realizing that it might be over
Hope the fear melts all the ice of stillness in ourselves
And you don't have to ask yourself what's left
Is there anything left how could I thought so much about it
maybe it was all supposed to fall like this
perhaps it was not, and we are still hearing things without
saying a thing

Chapter8

Things might not come easy it's hard at times
It might seem a never-ending quest
But it's strange to think that it may never change
Nothing is supposed to be there forever
Even all the golden era has passed
what you need to do is just stand till it passes
And do not try to look back how it passed
And those how are true will always stay.

Chapter9

Hope you can see this in your mind
Living the life you wanted living that in tranquillity
standing there for yourselves on your terms
leaving those behind who does not fit in that picture
Dont put this up for the next day
dont fear for it; you might stumble
fall and cry to prepare for it sometime
In the end, you will win from things you never thought you could
Hope you can live this with your eyes open.

Chapter10

All imperfect, all of us suffering from something or other
Lying in our bed thinking what might go wrong
Like the previous thing which might have gone wrong or haywire
Waking up again and doing the same thing again and again
All those moments and thoughts are more accurate than anything I know
Eating my head with all those moments which turn out try in my mind
Sitting here waiting for everything to fall in place
Sitting and realizing that everything is still changing and moving.

Chapter11

When everything's diminishes
and you feel so alone
At the point when the downpour doesn't stop
Furthermore, you can't make it home or your own
At the point when it feels you are going to be far away
What's more, you simply need to let it go
It can't rain for eternity
Yet you can't know actually for what
At the point when it looks like all your flaw
Simply hang tight with the way you are going
The daylight will come
The tempest consistently passes.
It won't keep going forever
The downpour constantly stops and offers an approach to a great climate.
The most splendid and hottest of days are still to come.
Kindly hang tight with the bit of light still there.

Chapter12

In all fakery of the world
where fakeness picks troubled mind making it harder to find
it seems like an endless maze where things might not fall into place
you might say hope is fiction, but deep down, it keeps you warm
You really dont know when it's going to end
All the fear you had come try, and now the new ones lie ahead
Dont expect yourself to be the glue of the broken glass
In all the fake enchantresses of the world, dont expect to fake yourself
To learn what you dont know,
To find new places and things which belongs to you
To find the peace and whatever it means to you
Could help you focus on this fake enchantress in the world.

Chapter13

Your fear is not surprising, It comes from experiences you
wish you never had
Those things which seem to be in your control but were not
Making you feel too little or too sad over all those things
Thinking about the doors which you went through and
found it nowhere to end
Ambition and goal might seem to be a little unachievable
Can we just sit and look at the moon changing its intensity
like sometimes we do
From there, look at the people who came, stayed and made
you feel what you want to feel,
Moon has seen all your despair, It has seen of everybody else
as well dont give up it will be okay.

Chapter14

We are all guests to a flawed society sometimes trying to move from a squared wheel
Trying to discover and dance from a scared and unjust world,
It looks like you might not be built for all these
We are not just our struggle and success.
This time no matter how significant or insignificant, it will end
We meet new people lost the old one to meet ourselves and find ourselves,
We don't know where we belong, but we can define where we are heading
Denting the square wheel to be a little better than yesterday

Chapter15

You were glad, and sometimes You were sad
It wasn't all acceptable. However, it wasn't all bad as well
You played with books and guitar and whatever else you love
You assembled yourself with whatever fantasies and stories you have
Investigating the ways and combining all those separate threads
Beliving all those threads will make sense someday
It's all going to be connected one day
It's all going to make you smile one day,

Chapter16

What's the best thing in the world? It's not what we see; it's what makes you,

Things that add sadness, Things that stares you will go away eventually

However, everything which stays makes you

Dont shed tears that do not make you

Dont let your head cling and drown with the thoughts and things that won't stay for you.

Try to win with those thoughts and things until you unclutch yourself with them.

Deal it like a plant whose growth you can't rush however, just nurture it

Remind yourself find yourself what makes you.

Chapter17

The deepness of your thoughts might be making you
confused
most of the time it looks you hear the unsaid
The traffic light, dust, the space, the look which you just got
every night which you seems they want to say, you hear it all
I sit and wonder with all my heart
Looking at the flowing water which keeps everything go
away with time
Realising that water is filling something, going somewhere
EXPANDING
you will, too just like water, Dont think too much when it
feels like.

Chapter18

Some say everything is there to change and everything will change,
Do the Laws of Nature, and its related science is ever going to change
Does whatever happened in the past ever going to change
In the world of temporary people and things, it might look like everything is spontaneous
Few moments always remain permanent. It's not the years or decades but those small few moments.
That unexpected moment with the most surprising results is what makes you permanent to yourself.
Those moments when you realise it's not permanent make you permanent for yourself in those journies.
It's where our life is made, and our future is defined; maybe today you find that moment.

Chapter19

What makes you think you are not enough,
What makes you think you dont have people around you
Is it the fear of being left out, failure or some past experience
Whether it is sad or sweet, why does it bother you now so much
Is there any light in all this darkness that you believe is coming
Is there anything about all those darkness that makes you feel inspired by yourself
Like at 4:00 AM in the morning, waking up realising it's hard to be said or done
Let you be the light that separates you from the darkness.

Chapter20

To let your walls down, allow yourself to be seen. I know how it looks
Spend most of the time thinking about the songs I played for you
If it's about all the small moments and efforts which sometimes make us insecure
Does sharing miseries add more miseries, or does it reduce it? What does it do
In this fast world, Let my mind wander around things of joy, love and things which I dont known
I dont know what I truly desire is good for me. Is it actually that I will genuinely desire
Whatever it is, let us find it out alone or together, but first let breakdown that wall
Let us remind each other we are on a experiment we might fall and learn.

Chapter21

With all the Tiring and Demanding days
With all the exhaustive times for yourself
Days in which you just wish to be alone
Time like this makes you feel reluctant about yourself
With all that happened in the past remains in past
With all that is coming in the future remain uncertain
Find the light in those exhaustive days in the present
Release the weight you are caring unnecessary once just to
realize you are carrying that.

Chapter22

Things are not sometimes what it looks like to us
There are things we learn and unlearnt every day
Why do we need to forget something and move on? Was not it our choice ones
Sometimes dont we just avoid the truth to not have those thoughts reappear
The world is there waiting for you
I wake and grin. My dreams are true
Thinking the chaos and fear will soon be gone miraculously
We are waiting for the perfect time for all this, which we dont believe could be now.

Chapter23

Days are there where only opposite of what we want happen
That's how we differentiate between a good and bad day
Not realizing those things which went wrong was never intended to be right
On the off chance that lone my mind could talk and express,
At that point, it could tell to you those bad days were more decisive than the good ones
As after a lot of storms, there is a rainbow to be seen in the sky
Whatever pain and scars had to heal, if you let them know what else they can do.

Chapter24

Today might be a little different
You might not have been truthful to yourself and stopped being you
There might be stories to say and things to tell
Now it looks like it was too much to take and too little to look
Currently there are journeys which you had brought which you never wanted to take
Today it might be not what it was yesterday
What you thought it could have been
It's slipping by, and that's there it will change.

Chapter25

The same morning, The same question what's there for today

Is it going to be like the guy sitting left a little sad reading something on his phone

The thing which I am so worried about is the people , ideas, things do that matter

Looking at him, it seems he is lost. The birds are chirping it's beautiful outside

I wanted to tell him to just look above. It's not that sad; there are childrens nearby

He seemed to have lot in his problem

What a beautiful day he will never know what he is missing

Looking below, I realise there is a notification on my phone.

Chapter26

I am so far off from the place and people where I feel I belong
All-weather and all the changes feel insignificant to me.
I am doing this is what's gonna happen even if I accomplish this.
I do ask these questions at times a lot of times.
Finding my own self in a world which seems to have changed
Finding the reason to still do what I once thought i was just made for
The desire to achieve what now I even dont care for
I wish I make this place where I belong as it was once.

Chapter27

Just consider how much you've accomplished in the past
How much you've learned, and how much you've grown
Is it essential to consider the items that were burned along the way?
NO! NO! The beauty is ahead of you, not in the time you've squandered.
With the same goal, we glance at the same moon and sky
The thoughts that came out of our heads are what draws you closer
You offer the calm that we so much require in these times
However, we must continue to improve and work hard along the road
For tomorrow to be better than today.

Chapter28

You are here,
It's not necessary, what we achieve ultimately
What's looks more interesting is the journey itself
It's not necessary to understand at first what's it all for
It's essential to understand each other at the time
It's Important to know what belongs to you
Those things which will be there no matter what
Dont keep things inside. Let it out
Say it what's needed, reflect yourself
Dont let others' anger be on your mind
Be accessible, and remember you are a priority always to yourself
You are here it is not necessary but looks more interesting the beautiful journey
What it is all about, At the time
Those things will never have to ask
Say it what needed Dont to let others bother you
Be free and remember you are the first priority to yourself.

Chapter29

Hello There,
What keeps you going every day
It is your drive that might keep you going
It is just being the desire of being happy
Over time and time
It might be the desire to keep loved ones delighted.
Whatever it is, You will soon realise it
Soon there than later
Some doors might close, and others might open
what is to remind there are more doors
Hello There, I hope you get your answers soon.

Chapter30

Just consider how much you've accomplished in the past
How much you've learned, and how much you've grown
Is it important to consider the items that were burned along the way?
NO! NO! The beauty is ahead of you, not in the time you've squandered
With the same goal, we glance at the same moon and sky
The thoughts that come out of your head are what draws you closer
you offer the calm that we so much need in these times
However, we must continue to improve and work hard along the road
In order for tomorrow to be better than today.

Chapter31

You might believe it or not
You can't see your way today, or its blur
You might not connect things; it might be all nuisance now
You have crossed a road that others might not see
It's all part of the journey. It's going to be worth it
You stand tall and can see in ways no one else can
You might not react, but you felt absolutely everything
The road to fulfilment is not straight, but it has checkpoint.

Chapter32

You must think that there is something lovely today
Leaving the past behind for the future that awaits us
we gaze at the same moon passing by day and night
hoping that our sacrifices will be repaid in full
Despite the hundreds of miles between u and your destiny
I never stop going forward in the same manner I always do
wishing for a bright future filled with an abundance of serenity and wisdom
Hope you are going places you never imagined you would go.

Chapter33

Be there for yourself, forever and ever
Doing things that might not matter
But do it because nobody will do it for you
For all the mistakes you ever made
Forgive yourself; life is supposed to be like that sometimes
What went wrong was not your fault
Don't go down with all the work you have
Just keep going for some time.

Chapter34

Good things come with time
It takes efforts, sacrifice and commitment
It is disheartening and scary at times
It will take work. It will take blood and sweat
It might take unwanted miseries and pain
It might never even happen
It might just be another attempt at failure
However, you will try again and again
Because good things come with time.

Chapter35

Some people will come and go, while others will stay
you may be harsh on yourself for judging something wrong
What's there to be concerned about it.
Some will stay, Some will not. Let's be there for those how
stayed
Trying to be the best version of ourselves
doing what is suitable for ourselves
And growing for ourselves and those all along
How Stayed.

Chapter36

It might not all be perfect and precise what's going on
What should remain is that smile & peace of mind
As the breeze and wave pass, those. self-doubts will pass
Giving way to all those scars left behind with a strong soul
you know very little, but the fact that you will grow is true
The fact that everything is gonna be what it meant to be accurate
Don't let yourself lose from within
When all seems to go wrong, just hang yourself there a bit more.

Chapter37

You don't need walls in your heart trying to crush you
What you need is an endless river overcoming all obstacles
We need distance to feel closer to ourselves sometimes
We need to be truthful to ourselves and just to ourselves
It's the shaky storms we need to go deeper into our thoughts
We don't need to hide our true selves to look sane
We need to know sacrifice what we have for what we want
Using the one and the only chance we have here to make it
worthwhile.

Chapter38

Hope everything is going great
Like a new life every day, little by little, going ahead
Take control and lead the way
With things you don't see with these eyes
But looking at them from inside, Knowing where to go
Some people remain alongside your good and bad
Through all that life tosses your direction
As we develop and grow, we will perceive
As for why everything occurs and be glad for that.

Chapter39

You must think that there is something lovely today
Leaving the past behind for the future that awaits us
we gaze at the same moon passing by day and night
hoping that our sacrifices would be repaid in full
Despite the hundreds of miles between u and your destiny
I never stop going forward in the same manner I always do
wishing for a bright future filled with abundance of serenity
and wisdom.
Hope you are going places you never imagined you would
go.

Chapter40

When everything seems fine, It still might be different
Where it looks that there is nothing to fear
You generally realize precisely what to state and do
Simply looking forward, looks it all joyful and bright
Choosing myself over the entire being
Behaving like it's never gonna end
Thus LAUGH, SMILE from Inside
We all need to be a little crazy in some way or another.

Chapter41

The day passed like any other one
You tried even a little bit that matters
You stood thinking about your good and bad
sometimes about the evil that lies in others
Knowing that expecting anything is wasteful
Learning to be independent is your key
Not thinking much about the future
We should think about how to build that future.

Chapter42

There are days good and evil,
There are days lonely and with nothing to look at
In this world, You might have to pretend to be numerous beings
Let it be what it is for some time; you can't let their jealousy control what you think
Discouragers can reveal to you that I won't
Regardless of what anyone says
you have faith in yourself
This all may take some time
But it's going to end on the FINISH LINE.

Chapter43

Don't let yourself down in pleasing others
It's not what you built for, made for or trained for
Say what you feel, act what you have and dream what you want
Don't be the chaos of your mind, don't kill your own ideas and strength
Sustainable Ideas are born inside deep breath, silence or with some peaceful
Don't try too hard to be hard. Don't try to be what you wish you are not
We might just try, try to be stupid, stubborn and whatnot, but it's going to be worth it.

Chapter44

I believe the upcoming day goes nice for you
I hope it remains that way forever
Without that ominous distraction
The silence which comes to you
Is that off tranquillity and fulfilment
Hope the days ahead
Brings you the same joy and love
Keeping yourself closer with yourself
Diminishing the Difference which you have with yourself
Making it a thing of past

Chapter45

Sometimes we fall, sometimes we succeed.
Sometimes we might have failed for others and ourselves
Sometimes you might have found yourself in darkness all alone
Sometimes it all seems so meaningless and flawed
At those times, I hope you find yourself with yourself
Without any doubt or resentment, you see the inner child
I believe it will work out better for you and all around
Just don't give up or doubt yourself.

Chapter46

Your destiny has chosen your way
You lose some, you win some
But your path is specific, it's all the work which you have done
Which tells you, you can do more when you accomplish all that
There have been a lot of thorns in your life
The flower in that thorn will bloom; just keep going
It's all gonna be worthwhile and fulfilled
Just be in Peace and give yourself some ease.

Chapter47

Your destiny has chosen your way
You lose some, you win some
But your path is specific; it's all the work which you have done
Which tells you, you can do more when you accomplish all that
There have been a lot of thorns in your life
The flower in that thorn will bloom; just keep going
It's all gonna be worthwhile and fulfilled
Just be in Peace and give yourself some ease.

Chapter48

You might want to go away to a far place
You might say a few things turned out differently
You might say a lot of people playing with you
I will say you are trying your best that's what matters
Things are not meant to be easy, but your journey is going to be worth it
I will say it's a new beginning, Everyday
Let's see will do at least something.

Chapter49

Few people are a gift from Heaven
Like on the darkest night, the brightest star appear
Those people are blessing and love
It's all the reason and more
We fight for things and moments
No matter how harsh it gets
We learn the true meaning
For what which issues and what which does not.

Chapter50

You might know all about me from inside and out
Looking at the same moon and sun every day
We took chances and risks for what we wanted to be
We knew all those would come true someday
As great things take time so, this might take so
Let's just move forward and move.

Chapter51

When we ourselves are tired, and it seems unending
We can't tell even people what it is
We admit and chucked all of it
We try to do the best for ourselves,
It might look it's constant and here to stay
But it won't
Your torment and throbs make it more stressful
This, too, will pass very soon.

Chapter52

Yes, things come and go
Almost all things arrive and depart
A very few of those things stay
Making it a joy forever
It then stays even when we don't want it to
Fighting for those sometimes unintentionally
Making us dependent and attached
Stick to those things which stayed.

Chapter53

Today is a new challenge
When challenges lurked inside your head
Often do we sideline our expectations
Look in the past of what you achieved
Let be like sand in the sea storm near the shore
Let it pass too
like all the previous challenges which came and went
Stand there for a little longer until it passes

Printed by Libri Plureos GmbH in Hamburg,
Germany